The Day
of the Lord

The
Day of the Lord

Brian K. McCallum

Sixth Printing 1998

ISBN 0-89276-950-5

Contents

Foreword

The title I have chosen for this book — *The Day of the Lord* — is significant, because it stands for the period of time the book covers.

Second Peter 3 speaks of events at (1) the end of the current Age of Grace as well as events (2) in the future Millennial Age.

For example, the events spoken of in verse 10 actually occur at the end of the Millennial Age, which is Christ's thousand-year reign upon the earth: "... *the heavens shall pass away with a great noise, and the elements shall melt with fervent heat, the earth also and the works that are therein shall be burned up.*"

Yet in this same verse, Peter, by inspiration of the Holy Spirit, called this present hour "the day of the Lord." We are prone to think that "the day of the Lord" refers to the day of Jesus Christ's Second Coming to establish that millennial kingdom on earth, and the phrase may be correctly used that way. But it also may be correctly used to refer to the events of the end of the present Age of Grace, including the "catching away" of the Church, which shortly precedes Jesus' Second Coming.

The Spirit of God gave us insight into this when He inspired Peter to record "... *one day is with the Lord as a thousand years, and a thousand years as one day*" (2 Peter 3:8).

Therefore, when we see the term "the day of the Lord" used in Scripture, we must decide from context and with the help of the Holy Spirit which period of time we are seeing. Remembering this, we look to the Word of God and the Holy Spirit to direct our path as we study the events of the end times.

I want to acknowledge several men of God whose writings and teachings have inspired and greatly helped me in my own study and the writing of this book: Rev. Kenneth E. Hagin, Rev. Ralph Mahoney, and Dr. Roy Hicks.

Rev. Brian K. McCallum
June 1985

Chapter 1
Rightly Dividing the Prophetic Word

Eschatology is the study of Bible prophecy and events past, present, and future predicted in the prophetic Scriptures. We would do well to see what the Bible itself has to say about the study of such Scriptures.

The Word tells us in John 16:13: *"Howbeit when he, the Spirit of truth, is come, he will guide you into all truth: for he shall not speak of himself; but whatsoever he shall hear, that shall he speak: and he will shew you things to come."*

This clearly tells us what believers can expect the Holy Spirit to do as we seek to have God-given understanding of the prophetic Word. There are not four or five different ways for these Scriptures to be interpreted, such as is now being done by well-meaning Christians. Rather, there is one way and only one way events will unfold to fulfill the Bible prophecies.

Just as Jesus Christ came in one place, at one time, to one people, in one city — all fulfilling prophecies about His first coming — so will end-of-the-age events unfold in *one* way.

Notice that the Word also said in John 16:13, *". . . and he will shew you things to come."* One way the Holy Spirit does that is by giving us His light on prophetic Scriptures.

But what is our part? How are we responsible? Second Timothy 2:15 gives us the answer: *"Study to shew thyself approved unto God, a workman that needeth not to be ashamed, rightly dividing the word of truth."*

Light, curious, intellectual, or feigned interest will not lead us to anything but confusion in any area of God's Word. The prophetic area is no different. We must *diligently* study the body of prophetic Scriptures and lean heavily on the guidance of the Holy Spirit if we hope to see future events as they actually will transpire. Then we will truly be workmen who need not be ashamed.

I can't think of anything more shameful than to attempt to predict a specific date when Jesus Christ will return. Do you know that *all* such predictions made heretofore have been proved to be false with the passage of time? I remember when one group took out a two-page ad in the Tulsa, Oklahoma, newspaper, predicting that Jesus would return on May 14, 1981. We know He didn't. We have reason to suspect anything else, including the preaching of the Gospel, that group might do. Such predictions bring shame on the Body of Christ, yet people continue to make them.

Jesus had something to say about this. We can see from what He said why we miss it when we attempt such predictions and why all such predictions are doomed to failure: "*. . . It is not for you to know the times or the seasons, which the Father hath put in his own power*" (Acts 1:7). Jesus said this to His disciples after they asked Him if He would, at that time, restore the kingdom to Israel. He also plainly told us it is not for us to know when His Second Coming will take place.

"*But of that day and hour knoweth no man, no, not the angels of heaven, BUT MY FATHER ONLY*" (Matt. 24:36). This passage comes right after Jesus taught that the regathered nation of Israel, prospering in their homeland, was a sign that the end of this age is near.

Do you agree that Jesus meant what He said? I believe you do. How futile it is, then, to try to figure out by *any means,* no matter how right or logical it may seem, what only the Father God Himself knows! Thank God we are delivered from such foolishness.

At this point, I want to answer some questions about what Jesus said concerning the end times. Let's begin with Matthew 24:

> MATTHEW 24:2,3
> 2 And Jesus said unto them, See ye not all these things? verily I say unto you, There shall not be left here one stone upon another, that shall not be thrown down.
> 3 And as he sat upon the mount of Olives, the disciples came unto him privately, saying, Tell us, when shall these things be? and what shall be the sign of thy coming, and of the end of the world?

First, the Greek word translated "world" at the end of the third verse is more accurately translated "age." We then see the questions asked mean: What will be the sign of the Second Com-

2   #1 Regathering of Israel – to their homeland
        (Restoration)

ing (and the end of the present Age of Grace Jesus was then ushering in)?

Jewish men asked these questions. Jesus was talking to *Jews* about the future of the *Jewish* nation. Thus, it is very important for us to see from this Olivet Discourse (also found in Luke 21 and Mark 13) that Jesus was not talking to the Church about the future of the Church. These Jewish disciples were not yet born again or filled with the Holy Spirit. They could not have understood or accepted that there was going to be an Age of Grace in which God would take a people for Himself out of Gentile nations.

The Jews' attitude toward the Gentile nations was wrong. God always had meant Israel to be a light and a blessing to all the world. He never had meant for the Jews to make a religion out of His Word, to isolate themselves from Gentiles, or to look upon Gentiles as inferior beings. But that is precisely what Israel did.

Do you remember Jonah? When the Father God sent him to prophesy to Nineveh, Israel's enemy, he didn't want to go. After some supernatural persuasion, he finally went and proclaimed the message God had given him.

Now, those Assyrians who lived in Nineveh were known for their brutality and meanness. Israel had suffered much at their hands. But when they heard Jonah, the man of God, proclaim, "Forty days and Nineveh shall be overthrown," they repented and turned from their evil ways — from the king right down to the last Ninevite!

That would be like your going to an enemy nation, preaching God's Word, and seeing them all repent and be saved. Hallelujah! We would certainly enjoy that, but Jonah didn't. Jonah 4:1 tells us, ". . . it *DISPLEASED Jonah exceedingly, and he was VERY ANGRY*." Why? Because he had a wrong attitude toward the Ninevites. He wanted God to destroy them. That, thank God, was not the will of Almighty God.

The same attitude toward Gentiles existed in Jesus' day, as we see in Matthew 15:21-28. The Syrophoenician (or Canaanite) woman in this story was a non-Jew, but she had heard of Jesus, and she believed God was good — both able and willing to deliver her daughter from the grip of Satan.

3

In this discourse, we see Jesus revealing what Jews thought of Gentiles: "... *I am not sent but unto the lost sheep of the house of Israel*" (v. 24). Then, after she persisted in faith and worship, He said, "*It is not meet* [fitting or suitable] *to take the children's bread, and to cast it to DOGS.*" The woman replied, "*Truth, Lord: yet the DOGS eat of the crumbs which fall from their masters' table.*" Jesus said she had great faith, and she received deliverance for her daughter.

The Jews looked down their noses at Gentiles and categorized them all the same — *as dogs!* We can see this same attitude from the actions of the disciples in verse 23: "... *And his disciples came and besought him, saying, Send her away; for she crieth after us.*"

Here was a distraught mother with a demon-possessed daughter. The disciples already were commissioned by Jesus to minister deliverance, but they said, in effect, "Send her away. She's bothering us!" Why? Because she was a Canaanite (Gentile)! No deliverance for the dogs!

These events in Jesus' ministry indicate the wide rift that then existed between Jews and Gentiles. As we look forward in time, we see that it was eight to ten years after the Resurrection before God dealt with the Apostle Peter, showing him by vision and ministry that it was God's will for Gentiles to come into the family of God. The account of Peter's vision and his ministry to Cornelius' household is found in Acts 10.

After Paul and Barnabas' first missionary journey, they, along with Peter, went to the chief Christians in Jerusalem and shared the mighty works God had wrought among the Gentiles. Acts 15 gives us this account of the council at Jerusalem, which was headed by the Apostle James. The Church leaders were able to agree that God is no respecter of persons. Most scholars agree that this council took place 20 to 21 years after Jesus' resurrection. Jewish tradition died slowly.

With these accounts in mind, we can readily see why the Lord Jesus said to His disciples in John 16:12, "*I have yet many things to say unto you, but ye cannot bear them now.*"

One of the things they were not ready to receive in their unregenerate state was that the Gentiles could be saved, becoming brothers and sisters in Christ to Jewish believers. More than likely, their retort would have been, "Brothers with the dogs? Never!" They were not ready to hear about the Church Age. Therefore, except in general terms, Jesus was not telling them about the Church Age in Matthew 24, Luke 21, or Mark 13.

There was a rift between the Jews + Gentiles
As far as Jews were concerned they were
Dogs - (wrong attitude) - But Jesus had
always wanted Israel to be a "light"
+ a "blessing" to all the world — So
he had to show Peter the vision
that it was Gods will that the
Gentiles come into the family also —
Salvation to Gentiles also

$300.00 - metal

150.00

500 bucks

Chapter 2
Israel in Prophecy

If Jesus was not describing the Church Age in Matthew 24, Luke 21, or Mark 13 (the Olivet Discourse), what *was* He talking about? He was addressing the questions He had been asked in Matthew 24:3. He was addressing these words to Jews who were not yet born again; He was telling them about the future of the nation of Israel. That is not to say that we find nothing relevant to the Church in these Scriptures; however, they are words spoken to Jews who did not know as yet there would even *be* a Church Age. We also see this in Acts 1:6. After Jesus' resurrection, these same disciples asked Him if He was going to establish His kingdom on earth at that time. They still had to learn there would be an Age of Grace.

With these things in mind, let us go through Matthew 24 and receive what God is saying about Israel's future and how it relates to believers now in the Church Age.

In verses four through eight, Jesus tells what will lead up to the end of the Age of Grace.

In verse five, He mentions deceivers who will even claim to be God's anointed, but who are not. He says they will deceive many. (Mohammed, Mary Baker Eddy, Sun Myung Moon, and others would fit that description and fulfill the prophecy.)

Verses 9 through 13 tell of the beginning and the intensifying of troubles for Israel predicted in Daniel 9:24-27.

Verse 14 tells of the mission of Jewish believers during the 70th week of Daniel's prophecy. By the grace and mercy of God, they will finish the preaching of grace *after* the Church of Jesus Christ has completed the main harvest. Their work could be compared to gleaning the fields after the harvest is complete. (Notice that their harvest field, like that of the Church's, is the whole world.)

Verse 15 marks the mid-point of Daniel's 70th week. There has been an interlude of nearly 2,000 years from the close of the 69th week, when Jesus Christ was crucified, to the opening of

7

the 70th week. In the first half of that 70th week (3½ years), Israel will be allied to a federation of Middle Eastern nations headed by a powerful statesman and military leader, the anti-Christ. In symbolic terms, Revelation 13 tells of that alliance and its leaders, the anti-Christ and the false prophet. Daniel 11:21-45 gives a parallel description of the rise and fall of the beast empire and the anti-Christ. I suggest you read both of these accounts in the *New American Standard Version* for clarity and accuracy.

In verse 15, Jesus speaks of a time Daniel and others predict when the anti-Christ will turn against Israel, persecuting her and all other believers living then with "great tribulation" (v. 21).

Verses 16 through 28 are specific warnings and instructions to Jewish believers who will be living in Israel when these things come to pass. God has prepared a place of refuge for them, and now they must flee by any means possible to that place.

Verses 19 and 20 bear this out. Why did He say, "... *pray ye that your flight be not ... on the sabbath ...*"? Because Jews trained in Orthodoxy must not travel more than 2,500 feet on a Sabbath day, and, as we have already seen, such ingrained traditions die hard. Where is that place of refuge? Look with me in Daniel 11:41.

The anti-Christ's empire will not include Edom, Moab, and the foremost of the sons of Ammon. Those ancient nations on the East and South of Israel are presently Jordan and part of Saudi Arabia. This is the area where God has provided a refuge for Jews who have studied the New Testament and will obey it. When they are safely in that place of refuge, Satan will tempt them to leave through false prophets. Therefore, Jesus plainly tells them what His Second Coming to establish the Kingdom of God on all the earth will be like, thus delivering these believing Jews from that temptation. Thank God that His Word is deliverance for His people!

Let us look now at Matthew 24:36-51. (I am deliberately bypassing verses 32 through 35, which we will study later.)

Verse 36 confirms that it is futile for *anyone* to attempt to predict what only the Father God knows. Mark 13:32 says it this way: "*But of that day and that hour knoweth no man, no, not the angels which are in heaven, neither the Son, but the Father.*"

8

We cannot know in advance, then, what the Father has reserved to Himself. I think that knowledge itself gives us great peace to be fully occupied today with the work of reconcilation as able ministers of the New Covenant.

Matthew 24:37-39 tells us: *"But as the days of Noe [Noah] were, so shall also the coming of the Son of man be. For as in the days that were before the flood they were eating and drinking, marrying and giving in marriage, until the day that Noe entered into the ark, AND KNEW NOT UNTIL THE FLOOD CAME, AND TOOK THEM ALL AWAY; so shall also the coming of the Son of man be."*

In these verses, Jesus is telling the disciples about an event connected with His Second Coming. Also, He is comparing that event to conditions in Noah's time, when the wicked, hard-hearted people were destroyed by the flood:

GENESIS 6:5-13
5 And God saw that the wickedness of man was great in the earth, and that every imagination of the thoughts of his heart was only evil continually.
6 And it repented the Lord that he had made man on the earth, and it grieved him at his heart.
7 And the Lord said, I will destroy man whom I have created from the face of the earth; both man, and beast, and the creeping thing, and the fowls of the air; for it repenteth me that I have made them.
8 But Noah found grace in the eyes of the Lord.
9 These are the generations of Noah: Noah was a just man and perfect in his generations, and Noah walked with God.
10 And Noah begat three sons, Shem, Ham, and Japheth.
11 The earth also was corrupt before God, and the earth was filled with violence.
12 And God looked upon the earth, and, behold, it was corrupt; for all flesh had corrupted his way upon the earth.
13 And God said unto Noah, The end of all flesh is come before me; for the earth is filled with violence through them; and, behold, I will destroy them with the earth.

From this passage we see that judgment from God was sent to the earth. The corrupt, wicked, hard-hearted, unrepentant sinners were removed, or "taken" from the earth. In other words, the natural human lives of these people came to an end. After the flood, only Noah and his family were left.

Let's relate that time to the time Jesus was talking about in Matthew 24. Remember, He said in verse 39, "... *so shall also the coming of the Son of man be.*" Therefore, if the evil and unrepentant were "taken" in Noah's day, they will be taken at Jesus' Second Coming. (By "Second Coming," we mean His coming to end Armageddon and to establish His kingdom on the earth.)

Be careful now. Don't forget whom Jesus was addressing. He was talking to Jews who were not yet born again and who didn't know there would even be an Age of Grace.

To shed more light on what Jesus was talking about, look at the parable of the wheat and the tares and its explanation, found in Matthew 13.

MATTHEW 13:24-30,36-43

24 Another parable put he forth unto them, saying, The kingdom of heaven is likened unto a man which sowed good seed in his field:

25 But while men slept, his enemy came and sowed tares among the wheat, and went his way.

26 But when the blade was sprung up, and brought forth fruit, then appeared the tares also.

27 So the servants of the householder came and said unto him, Sir, didst not thou sow good seed in thy field? from whence then hath it tares?

28 He said unto them, An enemy hath done this. The servants said unto him, Wilt thou then that we go and gather them up?

29 But he said, Nay; lest while ye gather up the tares, ye root up also the wheat with them.

30 Let both grow together until the harvest: and in the time of harvest I will say to the reapers, Gather ye together first the tares, and bind them in bundles to burn them: but gather the wheat into my barn.

Now look at verses 36-43. They contain Jesus' explanation of what this parable is all about. (Note especially verses 40,41.)

36 Then Jesus sent the multitude away, and went into the house: and his disciples came unto him, saying, Declare unto us the parable of the tares of the field.

37 He answered and said unto them, He that soweth the good seed is the Son of man;

38 The field is the world; the good seed are the children of the kingdom; but the tares are the children of the wicked one;

39 The enemy that sowed them is the devil; the harvest is the end of the world; and the reapers are the angels.
40 As therefore the tares are gathered and burned in the fire; so shall it be in the end of this world.
41 The Son of man shall send forth his angels, and they shall gather out of his kingdom all things that offend, and them which do iniquity;
42 And shall cast them into a furnace of fire: there shall be wailing and gnashing of teeth.
43 Then shall the righteous shine forth as the sun in the kingdom of their Father. Who hath ears to hear, let him hear.

Jesus was telling of the judgment that will come upon the *wicked* at the end of the age. This is very plain talk. It is impossible to misinterpret it. In verse 41, Jesus plainly said the angels will *gather out* of His kingdom all things that offend, *"and them which do iniquity."*

Now let's look at Matthew 24:40,41. Some will protest, "But I always thought this was talking about the rapture of the Church!" There *is* going to be a rapture of the church, but Jesus wasn't talking about that here. The Jews couldn't yet receive the fact of a Church existing from all nations, so Jesus wasn't telling them about the Church's future here. He was talking about Israel's future at the end of the age and the future of all the unbelieving at that time. We see clearly that the "taken" in verses 40 and 41 are the evil and unbelieving! (Yes, I realize that probably ruins some of our theologies. Some of them need to be ruined!)

Also notice, however, that there are those who are left. From Matthew 13 and other Scriptures, we can conclude that there will be human beings who will come out of the Great Tribulation and enter into the Millennial Kingdom. Zechariah 14:16 says, *"And it shall come to pass, that every one that is LEFT of all the nations which came against Jerusalem shall even go up from year to year to worship the King ..."*

By reading the context around this verse, you can see that the prophecy is talking about those who are "left" after the Battle of Armageddon, or after the Lord's Second Coming. In the Millennium, they will go up to Jerusalem annually to honor and worship Jesus. These natural humans will repopulate the earth during the thousand years, as we can see from Revelation 20:7-9: *"... the*

mill - 1,000 yr reign of christ

11

nations which are in the four quarters [the whole] of the earth . . ."

Who will they be? Who will be left? There is some light on this from several sources, but I think we can safely leave it in God's hands. We can be instructed as Samuel was when he went to anoint a king to reign over Israel: ". . . *for the Lord seeth not as men seeth; for man looketh on the outward appearance, but the Lord looketh on the heart*" (1 Sam. 16:7).

In Psalm 145:9 we read, "*The Lord is good to ALL: and his tender mercies are over ALL HIS WORKS.*" And verse 17 of the same Psalm tells us, "*The Lord is righteous in ALL his ways, and holy in ALL his works.*" He will direct this work, and the angels will do it in goodness, mercy, righteousness, and holiness.

There is another point to be made from Matthew 24:31, which says: "*And he shall send his angels with a great sound of a trumpet, and they shall gather together his elect from the four winds, from one end of heaven to the other.*"

Mark 13:27 says it this way: "*And then shall he send his angels, and shall gather together his elect from the four winds, from the uttermost part of the earth to the uttermost part of heaven.*"

God's elect who are in heaven and God's elect who are still on the earth will be gathered together at this time — the time of His Second Coming. Those who are in heaven will come *with* Him (Jude 14,15; Rev. 19:14), and those who have become believers during the Great Tribulation will be gathered *unto* Him to meet Him at His return.

During Christ millennium reign (1,000) there will be humans who will re populate the earth — Some of these (when Satan is loosed after the 1,000 yrs,) will rebel against God — By then we've been to heaven + are ruling w/christ zech 14:16 (in his 1,000 yr reign) says that those who survive the tribulation will come to Jerusalem to worship the King —

12

Chapter 3
The Sign of His Coming

In Matthew 24:3, the disciples asked Jesus, "... *and what shall be the sign of thy coming, and of the end of the world?*" We already have seen that the Father is the only one who knows the day and the hour. Now let's examine Jesus' answer:

> MATTHEW 24:32-35
> 32 Now learn a parable of the fig tree; When his branch is yet tender, and putteth forth leaves, ye know that SUMMER is nigh:
> 33 So likewise ye, when ye shall see all these things, know that IT is near, even at the doors.
> 34 Verily I say unto you, This generation shall not pass, till all these things be fulfilled.
> 35 Heaven and earth shall pass away, but my words shall not pass away.

First we need to recognize that Jesus inserts a parable here in verse 32 in the midst of the account of Israel in the last days. Remembering what parables are will help us to understand these verses. *Parables are stories or accounts told in symbolic language which represent truths, but they themselves do not literally tell the same truth.*

In this parable, Israel the nation is symbolized by the fig tree. There are many other instances in Scripture where this is also true: Mark 11:13,14,20-22 (the account of Jesus cursing the fig tree); Luke 13:6-9; 21:29-31, Jeremiah 24:1-10; Habakkuk 3:17; and Micah 4:4.

Reading further in the parable, we see that when the fig tree's branch is yet tender and young, putting forth its leaves, the time for it to bear fruit is near; that is, summer is at hand. Likewise, when we see all the things Jesus has been speaking of in this chapter coming to pass, we can know that the time for Israel to bear much fruit is at hand. In fact, we are told in verse 34 that *the generation which witnessess all these things, including the regathering of Jews in their homeland and the return of national Israel to the international scene, also will witness the Second*

Coming of Christ to rule and reign on earth.

Notice the parallel account of this in Luke 21:29-31 speaks, again in a parable, of *all the trees* putting forth foliage. This is the wave of nationalism that we clearly have seen in our time; especially since World War II.

The most important part of this is to see that the time for fruit is near. Israel, the nation that produced our Lord and Savior in the human sense, did not, as a whole, receive Him as the Messiah. However, the time for the Jews to receive Christ by the grace of God is very near or, as Jesus said in Matthew 24:33, ". . . *even at the doors.*"

The miracle of Israel's becoming a nation once again, despite opposition from nations that have arrayed themselves against God, is truly a great sign — a modern-day, Exodus-type miracle. It is what makes men *know* they are living in the final generation before Jesus' return.

From 70 A.D. until 1948, when the modern-day nation was proclaimed, the nation of Israel did not fully exist. If you follow current events, you know that this nation could not have survived without the repeated miraculous intervention of God. The 1973 Yom Kippur War comes to mind as the best example of these miracles. Egypt and Syria secretly and successfully staged a surprise attack on Israel while the Jews were celebrating their Day of Atonement. But, having gained the advantage of surprise and destruction of the Israeli outposts, both nations paused when they could have delivered Israel a death blow. This allowed Israel time to alert and regroup her defenses, go on the offense, and eventually gain the military victory.

That was a miraculous intervention by God. The enemies' pause could be compared to a soccer team's moving the ball down to the other team's goal area with only one defender between them and the goal, and then stopping and kicking the ball themselves back to midfield. That is a strange tactic to use in either soccer or military affairs, isn't it?

World events that are coming to pass have been surely predicted and already partially fulfilled, just as God's Word says. Look with me to Ezekiel 36. (To get the whole picture, I suggest you carefully read both chapters 36 and 37.)

In this passage, God, through the prophet Ezekiel, was predicting, point by point, that the nation of Israel would be regathered in the Jewish homeland and that the Jews would be preserved there by the mighty working of God:

EZEKIEL 36:8-11
8 But ye, O mountains of Israel, ye shall shoot forth your branches, and yield your fruit to my people of Israel; for they are at hand to come.
9 For, behold, I AM FOR YOU, and I WILL TURN UNTO YOU, and ye shall be tilled and sown:
10 And I will multiply men upon you, all the house of Israel, even all of it: and the cities shall be inhabited, and the wastes shall be builded:
11 And I will multiply upon you man and beast; and they shall increase and bring fruit: and I will settle you after your old estates, and will do better unto you than at your beginnings: and ye shall know that I am the Lord.

I can hear some say, "But don't you believe this applies to the Church today?" Yes, I surely do. But I also see it means literally what it is saying concerning national Israel. Many portions of prophetic or historical Scripture contain symbolic or figurative truths which do apply to the Church today. *God, who cannot lie, could not say things which could be interpreted literally unless they also had literal meaning!* Thus, we conclude that *figuratively* it applies to the Church today, and *literally* it applies to the restoration of Israel. This is the principle involved, and it needs to be clearly understood.

However, there is more involved than Israel's simply being regathered and prospering in the Jewish homeland. God said in Romans 11:26,27: *"And so all Israel shall be saved: as it is written, There shall come out of Sion the Deliverer, and shall turn away ungodliness from Jacob: For this is my covenant unto them, when I shall take away their sins."*

This refers to the acceptance of Jesus Christ as Lord and Savior by all Jews who will believe. This is what the prophet uttered in Ezekiel:

EZEKIEL 36:24-27
24 For I will take you from among the heathen, and gather you out

15

of all countries, and will bring you into your own land.
25 Then will I sprinkle clean water upon you, and ye shall be clean: from all your filthiness, and from all your idols, will I cleanse you.
26 A new heart also will I give you, and a new spirit will I put within you [born again — filled with the Holy Spirit]: and I will take away the stony heart out of your flesh, and I will give you an heart of flesh.
27 And I will put my spirit within you, and cause you to walk in my statutes, and ye shall keep my judgments, and do them [live a believing, sanctified life].

What a wonderful time to be alive! We can witness these truths alive in the Church today and know that Israel and all the nations of the earth will partake of the mercy of God by passing under the rod and entering into the New Covenant (Ezekiel 20:37).

ZECHARIAH 8:13,23
13 And it shall come to pass, that as ye were a curse among the heathen, O house of Judah, and house of Israel; so will I save you, and ye shall be a blessing: fear not, but let your hands be strong. . . .
23 Thus saith the Lord of hosts; In those days it shall come to pass, that ten men shall take hold out of all languages of the nations, even shall take hold of the skirt of him that is a Jew, saying, We will go with you: for we have heard that God is with you.

Hosea 6:11 is in agreement with Zechariah: *"Also, O Judah, he hath set an harvest for thee, when I returned the captivity of my people."*
In these verses, we see believing Jews finishing the work of preaching the Gospel as Jesus said they would in Matthew 24:14. Again, they will glean from the harvest field of the whole world. Their converts will be tribulation saints. We see the result of their ministry in Revelation 7:

REVELATION 7:9,13,14
9 After this I beheld, and, lo, a great multitude, which no man could number, of all nations, and kindreds, and people, and tongues, stood before the throne, and before the Lamb, clothed with white robes, and palms in their hands . . .
13 And one of the elders answered, saying unto me, What are these which are arrayed in white robes? and whence came they?
14 And I said unto him, Sir, thou knowest. And he said to me, These are they which came out of great tribulation, and have washed their robes, and made them white in the blood of the Lamb.

Remember the principle of interpretation: The God who cannot lie will not say things in the Word that can be interpreted literally *unless* there also is a literal fulfillment of that Word.

Chapter 4
The Church in Prophecy

As we now turn in our study to the Epistles, let us remind ourselves that these Epistles are letters to the Church written from 15 to 55 years after Jesus' resurrection. They were written to born-again, Spirit-filled believers who had grown and matured to the point where they could receive the truths set forth in them. We find God's major revelation for the Church in the Epistles. We should live in these letters without ignoring the rest of God's Word.

Time is moving swiftly, and our God is working powerfully in the lives of those who will yield to Him. The present-day Church — the called-out ones, members of the Body of Christ — is another great sign that the Lord soon will return. Not since the first century has there been such a *sustained, world-wide awakening* to God and His purposes as we are seeing now.

> 1 THESSALONIANS 4:13-18
> 13 But I would not have you to be ignorant, brethren, concerning them which are asleep, that ye sorrow not, even as others which have no hope.
> 14 For if we believe that Jesus died and rose again, even so them also which sleep in Jesus will God bring with him.
> 15 For this we say unto you by the word of the Lord, that we which are alive and remain unto the coming of the Lord shall not prevent them which are asleep.
> 16 For the Lord himself shall descend from heaven with a shout, with the voice of the archangel, and with the trump of God: and the dead in Christ shall rise FIRST:
> 17 THEN we which are alive and remain shall be caught up together with them in the clouds to meet the Lord in the air: and so shall we ever be with the Lord.
> 18 Wherefore COMFORT one another with these words.

We are encouraged, first, concerning those believers who have died a natural death. We have the confident hope that we will all be reunited on that wonderful day when Jesus comes for the Church. We know that those who have fallen asleep (died) in Christ are presently living (spirit and soul) with the Lord (2 Cor. 5:8). We also are told that they will accompany Him when He returns for those who are still living on the earth. Why will He bring them with Him? Turn to First Corinthians 15.

> **1 CORINTHIANS 15:50-53**
> 50 Now this I say, brethren, that flesh and blood cannot inherit the kingdom of God; neither doth corruption inherit incorruption.
> 51 Behold, I shew you a mystery; We shall not all sleep, but we shall all be changed.
> 52 In a moment, in the twinkling of an eye, at the last trump: for the trumpet shall sound, and the dead shall be raised incorruptible, and we shall be changed.
> 53 For this corruptible must put on incorruption, and this mortal must put on immortality.

All believers will not experience physical death. Jesus revealed this to Paul, who wrote it under the inspiration of the Holy Spirit.

Believers who are *alive* when Jesus returns will not experience physical death. Their bodies will be *changed* "in the twinkling of an eye" — the smallest fraction of time — into immortal, glorified bodies, like Jesus'.

The saints who *died* before this time will return with Jesus to receive their immortal bodies, which will be both *resurrected and changed.*

Notice there is a sequence to this: First, the *dead* will be *reunited* with their *new body,* and they will rise. Then, those who are *alive* on the earth at Jesus' coming will be *changed* and will rise, and we will all meet the Lord in the air. Our bodies, whether living or dead, will be changed so quickly that the time it will take cannot be measured.

I firmly believe that this catching away of the saints will be witnessed by those living on the earth. Why do I say that? I say that as a result of studying every case where the Bible tells about those who were translated or caught up bodily. Let's look at them.

We'll start with Enoch. Genesis 5:24 says, *"And Enoch walked with God: and he was not; for God took him."*

The point is that someone knew Enoch had been caught up by God, so there must have been at least one witness. (How did they know that he didn't just fall into a tar pit?)

Elijah is the next case. In Second Kings 2:11,12 we read, "...
*and Elijah went up by a whirlwind into heaven. And Elisha saw
it...*" That was another translation that was witnessed.

The next incident concerns Jesus' death and resurrection. This
is found in Matthew 27:50-53. "*Jesus, when he had cried again
with a loud voice, yielded up the ghost... and the earth did quake,
and the rocks rent; and the graves were opened; and many bodies
of the saints which slept arose, and came out of the graves after
his resurrection, and went into the holy city* [Jerusalem], *and
appeared unto many.*" This refers to Old Testament saints in
Paradise who awaited Christ's finished work and who were then
caught up with Him into heaven.

In Acts 1:2, we read, "*Until the day in which he was taken
up...*" Then, in verse 9, we read, "*And when he had spoken these
things, WHILE THEY BEHELD* ["they" being the company of
believers], *he was taken up; and a cloud received him out of their
sight.*" Again, a witnessed translation. Are there more?

Yes. Look in Revelation 11:11,12. "*And after three days and
an half the Spirit of life from God entered into them, and they
stood upon their feet; and great fear fell upon them which SAW
them. And they heard a great voice from heaven saying unto them,
Come up hither. And they ascended up to heaven in a cloud; AND
THEIR ENEMIES BEHELD THEM.*"

These are the two witnesses of the Great Tribulation, and, true
to form, their translation is witnessed. That is why I believe the
departure of the Church also will be witnessed. It will be the last
great testimony of a victorious, overcoming, fully obedient Church
to worldly, Thomas-type people who must see in order to believe.

Chapter 5
Another Sign of His Coming

In this chapter, we will pause in our trip through the Scriptures to expound upon an important point.

The Word has shown us that national Israel has been regathered in her ancient homeland for the purpose of glorifying God. This is a great sign that we are near the end of the present age. There is, however, *another* great sign that the Lord is nearly ready to return. What is that?

The Church of the Lord Jesus Christ, the Body of Christ, also reveals the progress of God's work of redemption.

> EPHESIANS 4:11-13
> 11 And he gave some, apostles; and some, prophets; and some, evangelists; and some, pastors and teachers;
> 12 For the PERFECTING of the saints, for the work of the ministry, for the edifying of the body of Christ:
> 13 Till we all come in the unity of the faith, and of the knowledge of the Son of God, unto a PERFECT man, unto THE MEASURE OF THE STATURE OF THE FULNESS OF CHRIST.

Therefore, we see that the Church will reveal maturity "unto the measure" of Jesus Christ Himself! (The word translated "perfect" in these verses is better understood "maturity.") In the fifth chapter of Ephesians you will see that the Lord is coming for just that kind of Church — one without spot or wrinkle:

> EPHESIANS 5:25-27
> 25 Husbands, love your wives, even as Christ also loved the church, and gave himself for it;
> 26 That he might sanctify and cleanse it with the washing of water by the word,
> 27 That he might PRESENT IT TO HIMSELF A GLORIOUS CHURCH, not having spot, or wrinkle, or any such thing; but that it should be holy and without blemish.

To understand this verse in its full light, think of a family. God is comparing the Church with a family. In a family, there are mature members and immature members. The ones who are not yet mature are guided and blessed by those who already are full-grown and mature.

Jesus is coming for a Church that, as this verse says, is *glorious.* It also is a Church that will demonstrate true unity in the Spirit. Members of His Body will love one another selflessly, demonstrating the love of God and, thereby, the power of God to the whole world.

We have a part to play in achieving this. In the next chapter, we will examine in detail what God's Word says about our preparation for the great events when Jesus first comes for the Church and later comes to establish His kingdom on this earth.

Webster's dictionary defines the word "posterity" as follows: (1) all of a person's descendants, (2) all future generations. I want to point out what the Scriptures teach concerning two great posterities that have come from Abraham.

GENESIS 22:16-18

16 And said, By myself have I sworn, saith the Lord, for because thou has done this thing, and hast not witheld thy son, thine only son:

17 That in blessing I will bless thee, and in multiplying I will multiply thy seed as the stars of the heaven, and as the sand which is upon the sea shore; and thy seed shall possess the gate of his enemies;

18 And in thy seed shall all the nations of the earth be blessed; because thou hast obeyed my voice.

Notice that God promised Abraham that he would multipy two posterities to him. One, *"the stars of the heaven,"* are the *spiritual* posterity, or those who have believed as Abraham did. They are represented by a heavenly symbol, a star, because they are of the Spirit, and are God's spiritual heritage as well as Abraham's. (Galatians 3:29 also refers to this *believing* heritage when it says, *"And if ye be Christ's, then are ye Abraham's seed, and heirs according to the promise.")*

The other heritage, *"the sand which is upon the seashore,"* indicates Abraham's *natural* posterity. They are represented by an earthly, or natural, symbol of sand:

HEBREWS 11:12

12 Therefore sprang there even of one, and him as good as dead, so many as the STARS of the sky in multitude, and as the SAND which is by the sea shore innumerable.

So there are generations descended from Abraham by faith because they believed God, and there are generations descended from Abraham naturally; but they did not necessarily believe God as he did, as indicated in Romans:

ROMANS 9:27

27 Esaias [Isaiah] also crieth concerning Israel, Though the number of the children of Israel be as the sand of the sea, a remnant shall be saved.

Here the natural posterity (Jewish) is referred to when Paul writes that a remnant of the natural descendants of Abraham will be saved. That could not possibly be referring to the spiritual posterity, "the stars of the heaven." They *all* are saved, because they do believe and are Abraham's spiritual seed, having descended from Abraham, Isaac, Jacob . . . and Jesus Christ.

ROMANS 11:1

1 I say then, Hath God cast away his people? God forbid. For I also am an Israelite, of the seed of Abraham, of the tribe of Benjamin.

In this verse, Paul obviously is referring to the natural heritage, or posterity, of which he was a member. We know from all his testimony that Paul was as saved as a person can be. Therefore, he was a member of both posterities. That is possible, and it has been happening to Jews who have believed ever since Abraham's time. I, personally, am a believer and a member of the spiritual posterity, because I am Christ's. As far as I know, however, I am not a natural descendant of Abraham.

ROMANS 11:26

26 And so ALL Israel shall be saved: as it is written, There shall come out of Sion the Deliverer, and shall turn away ungodlinesss from Jacob.

This Scripture says *all* Israel shall be saved. Romans 9:27 said "... a remnant shall be saved." Confusing? Not if you apply what we've just learned about the two posterities.

All who believe will be saved. From the natural posterity (Jewish people and others who have descended from Abraham), a remnant will believe. Actually, that is true of every nation, for God has said that He will take a people for Himself "... *out of every kindred, and tongue, and people, and nation*" (Rev. 5:9).

So God does not have a "favored nation" policy. Instead, He has told us with absolute truth and amazing detail how He will deal with *one* nation, Israel, thereby showing us His heart and will for *all* nations.

Everyone who believes is the seed of Abraham, as Galatians 3:29 states. Let's look back to our earlier Scripture in Genesis 22:18, which says, "*And in thy seed shall all the nations of the earth be blessed; because thou hast obeyed my voice.*"

Since we believers know we are the seed of Abraham, we also know we are a blessing to every nation on the earth. (God said we are; therefore, there must be the manifestation of what He said.) In Matthew 5:13,14, Jesus said believers are "the salt of the earth" (a preservative) and "the light of the world" (driving out darkness). Verse 15 of the same chapter tells us; "*Neither do men light a candle, and put it under a bushel, but on a candlestick; and it giveth light unto all that are in the house.*"

Praise God, we have an effect on *all* in the house of humanity by being saved, born again, filled with the Holy Spirit, and yielded to our heavenly Father.

As you intercede and pray, as you share Jesus Christ, and as you live your life in Him, you are preserving the world from destroying itself! You are enlightening men's lives to cause them to turn to Christ. You are the *glorious* Church for whom Jesus said He would return. Thanks be to God who *always* causes us to triumph!

Chapter 6
The Glorious Church

Let us continue our study of God's dealings with the Church by looking at the Gospel of John:

> JOHN 15:15
> 15 Henceforth I call you not servants; for the servant knoweth not what his lord doeth: but I have called you friends; for all things that I have heard of my Father I have made known unto you.
> JOHN 13:34
> 34 A new commandment I give unto you, That ye love one another; as I have loved you, that ye also love one another.
> JOHN 15:14
> 14 Ye are my friends, if ye do whatsoever I command you.

Whatsoever we are commanded! That's very simple — that we love one another!

If we keep this commandment of the Lord Jesus Christ, we are His friends. And because we are His friends, He has promised to share with us all He has heard His Father say. That is *good news!* We are to know what God is doing in the earth because we are members of the Body of Christ. It isn't likely that He could do anything without His Body cooperating with its Head and accomplishing what the Head directs.

You will remember that God called Abraham His friend (James 2:23) and revealed to him what He was about to do in the earth concerning Sodom and Gomorrah (Gen. 18:17-33).

This is an unshakable principle of God. He works in the earth through people who believe Him — overcomers, doers of His Word. This principle will hold true concerning gathering in the end-time harvest the Word promises in Revelation 5:9,10: "... *for thou wast slain, and hast redeemed us to God by thy blood out of every kindred, and tongue, and people, and nation; And hast made us unto our God kings and priests: and we shall reign on the earth.*"

It is the will of God to perfect the saints for the work of the ministry (Eph. 4:12). The greatest work of the Church, the Body of Christ, remains to be done: to take a people for God out of every nation, people, tongue, and kindred. "Every" *means* every: *Every* nation on this earth, *every* remote tribe, will be visited by people with the Good News before Jesus comes for the Church.

Preparation for this great work is going on *now,* and reports from all over the world tell us that the harvest is beginning. The work of preparation in the Church must be completed first, or some of that harvest could be lost. When it is harvesttime, the farmer who is wise works with *all* his might until the harvest has been gathered in. Can we in the Church today, blessed abundantly by our Lord Jesus Christ, do any less? I think not!

Look with me at Revelation 3:21 and Revelation 19:7,8. These two passages portray the Church, which has obeyed the will of God:

> **REVELATION 3:21**
> 21 To him that overcometh will I grant to sit with me in my throne, even as I also overcame, and am set down with my Father in his throne.
> **REVELATION 19:7,8**
> 7 Let us be glad and rejoice, and give honour to him: for the marriage of the Lamb is come, and his wife hath made herself ready.
> 8 And to her was granted that she should be arrayed in fine linen, clean and white: for the fine linen is the righteousness of saints.

The New American Standard Bible and most other translations render the last phrase of Revelation 19:8 as, "the righteous acts of the saints."

In the above passages, we see believers who have fulfilled God's will *in* and *through* their lives in the earth. Remember, here and now is the only opportunity you ever will have to overcome! The world, the flesh, and the devil will not be present in the Millennium as far as you are concerned. *Now* is the time to overcome. *"And they overcame . . . by the blood of the Lamb, and by the word of their testimony . . ."* (Rev. 12:11).

There is nothing to overcome in heaven, nor will there be in all of God's creation for all of eternity. If we are to rule and reign with Jesus Christ for all eternity, we should begin to learn how to do so in this lifetime!

The Apostle Paul stated in the latter portion of his Christian life, *"Not as though I had already attained, either were already perfect: but I follow after . . . Brethren, I count not myself to have apprehended: but this one thing I do, forgetting those things which are behind, and reaching forth unto those things which are before, I press toward the mark for the prize of the high calling of God in Christ Jesus"* (Phil. 3:12-14).

Paul, by inspiration of the Holy Spirit, was telling us he was ever growing in grace; ever learning and increasing in the knowledge of God. He was on the upward path to final and total union with his Lord and Master, Jesus Christ. We learn from other Scriptures that Paul said he was running his race with all of his careful, steady effort. All the things of this world were counted loss by him that he might be totally pleasing to the One who called him to run.

Brothers and Sisters, we are running that same race, and, like the Apostle Paul, we are confident that Jesus' grace and love will insure that we finish our course with joy!

Revelation 19:7,8 shows us the picture of saints who, like Paul, have overcome to the fullest extent provided by the grace of God and have come to the place of total union with their Lord and Savior. What a happy day!

Jesus gave us the commandment to love one another, which we already have seen in John 13:34. It is love that will put us over and make us winners in the good fight of faith. Why? Because love is the most powerful spiritual force in the universe. God is love, and love *never* fails. As Galatians 5:6 tells us, faith works by love. In other words, faith gets its force, power, and strength from love.

This is the one commandment that Jesus the Creator of the whole universe gave us. He knew we needed something in this life that wouldn't crumble; He knew that love *never* fails. Love acted on is never in vain! It must bring forth a crop. Love is the means by which the Lord's prayer for us in John 17:21-23 could be answered: *"That they all may be one* [in agreement]; *as thou, Father, art in me, and I in thee, that they also may be one in us: THAT THE WORLD MAY BELIEVE THAT THOU HAST SENT ME. And the glory which thou gavest me I have given them; that they may be one* [in agreement], *even as we are one:*

I in them, and thou in me, that they may be made perfect in one; and that the world may know that thou hast sent me, and hast loved them, as thou hast loved me."

Jesus wants the world to know that the Father sent Him, that we are His disciples, and that the Father loves us as He loves Jesus. The only way this can happen is if we abide in something that never fails. If we are doers of love, we will never be failures!

The world will know that we are Jesus' disciples when the works of Jesus are in great manifestation. Faith will not be a problem when love is the rule of life. Just as faith is made perfect with corresponding actions, love is made perfect with corresponding actions. The spiritual man can grow up quickly when abiding in love.

Supernatural works have to be built on a supernatural foundation. To act in love is supernatural. To act contrary to love is natural, but Jesus said in John 6:63, *"It is the spirit that quickeneth* [makes alive]; *the flesh* [carnal senses] *profiteth nothing: the words that I speak unto you, they are spirit, and they are life."*

In First Corinthians 12, the manifestations of the Holy Spirit are mentioned. Verse 11 states, *"But all these worketh that one and the selfsame Spirit, dividing to every man severally AS HE WILL."*

With whom will He be pleased to divide His gifts? First John 4:16 says, *". . . God is love; and he that dwelleth in love dwelleth in God, and God in him."* It's the person who believes and acts on the Word who will cause the gifts of the Spirit to be brought into manifestation.

First Corinthians 12:31 tells us: *"But covet earnestly the best gifts: AND YET SHEW I UNTO YOU A MORE EXCELLENT WAY."* The next chapter of First Corinthians tells me that without love I'm a loud noise — I am nothing, and I profit nothing! Jesus said the flesh profits nothing; it's useless. He told us elsewhere in the Word that things highly esteemed among men are an abomination in the sight of God! No matter what the appearance may be — how good, noble, or wonderful — *God looks on the heart.*

There are no righteous acts apart from a heart motivated by

love. If I really earnestly desire spiritual gifts from the heart, I'll prove it by letting the law of love rule my life. If the desire for spiritual gifts is just to gratify the senses, that is not love, and there will be no manifested gifts of the Spirit of God. Again, *love works must be built on a love foundation.*

To abide in love is to know the Lord progressively from faith to faith and from glory to glory. We are conformed to His image as we grow in the knowledge of Him by hearing and acting on His Word. *Jesus and His Word are one.*

Master love, and you will not be lacking in anything in this lifetime or when you finally stand in the presence of God to receive your rewards. You will rejoice as did the Apostle Paul in Second Timothy 4:6-8: "... *the time of my departure is at hand. I have fought a good fight, I have finished my course, I have kept the faith: Henceforth there is laid up for me a crown of righteousness, which the Lord, the righteous judge, shall give me at that day: and not to me only, but unto all them also that love his appearing.*"

See yourself standing before Jesus to receive the rewards of faithfulness and love. Keep looking unto Him, the author and finisher of our faith.

Chapter 7
The Salt of the Earth

We have studied the Word concerning the end-time Church, that army of God marching in harmony and obedience to the Head of the Church, Jesus Christ. We now turn to a fundamental truth of the end times that is borne out by the Great Commission (Mark 16:17): *"And these signs shall follow them that believe; In my name shall they cast out devils ..."*

In Jesus' Name, believers will cast out the devil and all that pertains to him, praise God! For any anti-Christ to overpower the Church, God would have to issue Amendment One to the Gospel of Mark! He is *not* going to do that. His Word already is settled in heaven, and the overcoming Church is settling it equally on the earth as she fulfills that Great Commission.

Remember, the Great Commission is to preach the Gospel to every creature and fulfill what God has said concerning this present age: *"Simeon [Peter] hath declared how God at the first did visit the Gentiles, to take out of them a people for his name"* (Acts 15:14).

That is our job in this present dispensation. We are not told to turn the world into a paradise. (That is the work of the next age, the Millennium, when Jesus Christ will reign supreme on the earth.) *Now* in this hour, we are to be His witnesses in word, deed, and action. This will cause Jesus to be lifted up, and all who will to come to Him.

Now turn to our text:

2 THESSALONIANS 2:1-8
1 Now we beseech you, brethren, by the coming of our Lord Jesus Christ, and by our gathering together unto him,
2 That ye be not soon shaken in mind, or be troubled, neither by spirit, nor by word, nor by letter as from us, as that the day of Christ is at hand.
3 Let no man deceive you by any means: for that day shall not come, except there come a falling away first, and that man of sin be revealed, the son of perdition;
4 Who opposeth and exalteth himself above all that is called God,

or that is worshipped; so that he as God sitteth in the temple of God, shewing himself that he is God.

5 Remeber ye not, that, when I was yet with you, I told you these things?

6 And now ye know what withholdeth that he might be revealed in his time.

7 For the mystery of iniquity doth already work: only he who now letteth will let, until he be taken out of the way.

8 And then shall that Wicked be revealed ...

The Apostle Paul, by inspiration of the Holy Spirit, is imploring, or earnestly calling, on the believers in Thessalonica to understand facts concerning (1) the Second Coming of the Lord, and (2) our gathering together unto Him. He shows us in this passage how these two events relate to each other and how the latter opens the way for the former. He admonishes us to not be deceived by false doctrine, but to be at peace because of what we *know* is true concerning the future.

Read the whole passage again and read verse 15 through 17 of the same chapter. These verses give the true purpose of teaching on the end times: to establish, settle, and comfort believers concerning the events yet to come.

Verse 3 tells us that the coming of Jesus Christ to rule and reign on the earth will not come *until* some other event occurs first. Here it is translated "a falling away." It will allow the man of sin (anti-Christ) to be revealed. Verse 4 then tells us what the anti-Christ will do when he is revealed. In verse 5, Paul reminds believers he already had told them this part of his revelation when he was with them.

Now look closely at verses 6 and 7. They repeat the same truth told in verse 3. Paul says that now you know what is withholding the anti-Christ from being manifested. He then goes on to tell us that the mystery of iniquity is already at work. The Apostle John agrees with this in First John 4:3: "... *and this is that spirit of antichrist, whereof ye have heard that it should come; and even now already is it in the world.*"

Actually, that spirit has been in the world since the Garden of Eden. However, both these passages tell us there will be a *greater* manifestation of that evil spirit at some future time.

The key to the proper understanding of our entire text is found in Second Thessalonians 2:7: *". . . only he who now letteth will let, until he be taken out of the way."*

The Greek word translated here "letteth" and "will let" is the word translated "withholdeth" in verse 6: *katecho.* In other words, we could accurately say, "you know who is withholding anti-Christ . . ." and "he who is withholding anti-Christ will continue to do so until he is taken out of the way." Then and only then will that wicked (anti-Christ) be revealed whom or Lord Jesus will destroy with the brightness of His Second Coming.

Now look at verse three to get the proper sense of what is translated "falling away." The Greek word here translated "falling away" is *apostasia.* Used twice in the New Testament, its only other use is in the Book of Acts, where it means "to depart from the truth."

The root word for *apostasia* is *aphistemi,* which is generally translated "departed" or "departing from" in its many New Testament uses. Now read the verse with that understanding. You can clearly see that what it is saying is in perfect agreement with verses six and seven: The Second Coming of Jesus Christ will not take place *until* there is first a great *departure,* which allows the man of sin to be revealed!

Departure of what? By now, it should be plain that *it is the departure, or "catching away" (rapture), of the Church.*

Some would say, "I thought 'he' meant the Holy Spirit." The Church, the Body of Christ, can be referred to as "he" and is in this case. (The Church is referred to as a "perfect man" in Ephesians 4:13.) In many places, the Church is referred to as the "Body of Christ." Therefore, we see that it is not wrong to refer to the Church as "he."

Beyond that, the Holy Spirit is omnipresent in the world. We know this from other Scriptures:

PSALM 139:7-10
7 Whither shall I go from thy spirit? or whither shall I flee from thy presence?
8 If I ascend up into heaven, thou art there: if I make my bed in hell, behold, thou art there.

9 If I take the wings of the morning, and dwell in the uttermost parts of the sea;
10 Even there shall thy hand lead me, and thy right hand shall hold me.

The spirit of anti-Christ is currently being manifested more strongly in some parts of the world than others. Why? The difference lies in where the Church of the Lord Jesus Christ is in strong manifestation, filled with and empowered by the precious Holy Spirit of God.

"Ye are the salt of the earth," Jesus said in Matthew 5:13. One characteristic of salt — and the main use of it in Jesus' time — was to preserve foodstuffs. Jesus was saying to believers, "You are preserving the earth," or holding evil in check. There are many ways we manifest this; none is more important than prayer and intercession.

Chapter 8
The Overcomer's Prayer Life

Because prayer and intercession are such important parts of the work of the Church today, let us study the elements of prayer that are vital to the overcomer's prayer life. (Prayer is part of what makes the glorious Church glorious and the salt of the earth.)

The first thing God's Word admonishes us to pray for is found in First Timothy:

> 1 TIMOTHY 2:1-4
> 1 I exhort therefore, that, FIRST OF ALL, supplications, prayers, intercessions, and giving of thanks, be made for all men;
> 2 For kings, and for all that are in authority; that we may lead a quiet and peaceable life in all godliness and honesty.
> 3 For this is good and acceptable in the sight of God our Saviour;
> 4 Who will have all men to be saved, and to come unto the knowledge of the truth.

It isn't possible to expound at this time on all the truths in this passage. What we need to understand now is that we are told to pray *first* for those in authority. The purpose for our praying is for men to live in peace and to be saved. In other words, our prayers will create an atmosphere for the Gospel to go forth freely and be received.

Second, God's Word instructs us to pray for ministers of the Gospel, one another, and all saints. We could sum that up by saying, "the members of the Body of Christ," as seen in Ephesians 6:18: *"Praying ALWAYS with all prayer and supplication in the Spirit, and watching thereunto with all perseverance and supplication for ALL saints."*

Luke 18:1 reminds us that *"men ought ALWAYS to pray, and not to faint"* (give up). We also are exhorted to use all manner of prayer and supplication in the Spirit. We are to be alert to the guidance of the Holy Spirit to pray in tongues and with our understanding for *all* saints.

When you consider how vast the Body of Christ has become, you can see that the only way for *all* saints to be prayed for, or interceded for, would be as the Holy Spirit leads all members of the Body.

Third, we want to look at a specific type of prayer which is indigenous to the present age. This is the age when God's Word teaches us to pray as seen in James 5:7: *"Be patient therefore, brethren, unto the coming of the Lord. Behold, the husbandman* [Father God] *waiteth for the precious fruit of the earth, and hath long patience for it, until he receive the early and latter rain."*

With that verse in mind, look at Hosea 6:3: *"THEN shall we know, if we follow on to know the Lord: his going forth is prepared as the morning; and he shall come unto us as the rain, as the latter and former rain unto the earth."*

"Then" refers to an appointed time when this verse will be fulfilled. Notice that we of this generation will know only *"if we follow on to know the Lord."* That means to know His Word, doesn't it? We also see that this time will come just as surely as morning follows night. It has been thousands of years since Hosea prophesied it, but this prophecy is sure, because it is the Word of God! (Remember Second Peter 3:8, *". . . one day is with the Lord as a thousand years, and A THOUSAND YEARS AS ONE DAY."*)

Therefore, we are confident He will come to us as both the former and latter rain unto the earth. Well, what does "as the latter and former rain unto the earth" mean?

Looking at Deuteronomy 11:13-15, we find that God promised Israel He would send both first (former) rain and latter rain for their crops. The *former* rain was to prepare the ground for the planting and germination of the seed. The *latter* rain was to come prior to the harvest to give a full yield and a greater harvest.

The verses we are studying compare the end-time harvest of souls to this early and latter rain. In other words, God sent the Holy Spirit to begin the work, and there will be a latter-day manifestation of the Holy Spirit to fulfill and provide for a great, full, and final harvest of the precious fruit of the earth. What *is* the precious fruit of the earth? People! Human beings! For them, God gave *everything* He had: the precious life and blood of our Lord Jesus Christ!

How do we, by prayer, bring the latter-rain harvest to pass?

We have previously mentioned two areas: (1) intercession for those in authority, and (2) intercession for members of the Body of Christ.

Zechariah 10:1 mentions a third area: "ASK YE of the Lord rain IN THE TIME OF THE LATTER RAIN; so the Lord shall make bright clouds, and give them showers of rain, to every one grass in the field."

We, the called-out ones, the Body of Christ, are to *ask* of the Lord rain in the time of the latter rain. *This is that time!* We know to ask because we know Him and we know His Word, which is His will.

Today there are groups of believers who meet regularly and ask God for the manifestation of the latter rain. The Bible teaches us to "... ask, and ye shall receive ..." (John 16:24).

The Lord is making bright clouds today — saints who are doers of His Word — overcomers who will be greatly used of God to finish the work of the end times.

Are you yielding your life to our great God? Are you in God's perfect will for your life? Take time to talk to the Lord and be sure you are hearing Him. Then all that remains is for you to do as He has said.

As the Apostle Paul said, *"Wherefore comfort one another with these words"* (1 Thess. 4:18).

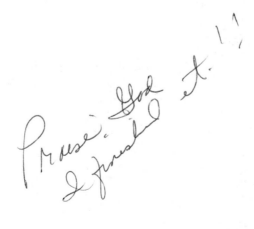